Forget Kids – Get a Dog

BY ALEX HALLATT

Copyright © 2019 by Alex Hallatt

Published by Moontoon Publishing

All rights reserved. No part of this book may be reproduced in any form or by any electronic or mechanical means, including information storage and retrieval systems, without written permission from the author, except for the use of brief quotations in a book review.

First Edition

ISBN: 978-0-473-48857-4

alexhallatt.com

For Billie.

We miss you, Bill.

CONTENTS

Introduction 5

Baby vs. Dog 9

Toddler vs. Dog 31

Schoolkid vs. Dog 55

Teenager vs. Dog 81

Epilogue 105

About the Author 109

Also by Alex Hallatt 110

INTRODUCTION

Kids are great. When they are well behaved and belong to other people. When you can play with them and their marble runs and hand them back before tears set in. When you can treat them to ice creams, but you don't have to pay for them to go to university. When you can read them a bedtime story, but don't have to go near them when they are hosting a mucus-borne, highly contagious disease.

Having children made sense in the days before social security, pensions and retirement homes. Children were slave labour on your farm or in your factory and it was worth having more than a couple, as few of them survived into adulthood. When you became too old to work for yourself, they took on more of the burden and looked after you too. Now they are more likely to sell your house, put you in a home and visit you as little as their conscience allows. And you wouldn't expect or ask otherwise.

Things have changed. You don't need children to inherit the farm (if you have a farm, they probably don't even want it). You can look after yourself in old age, or the State might do it for you. But you can't rely on children now. Best not to bother with children and get a companion you can rely on until the end of their days.

Forget kids — get a dog.

Baby vs. Dog

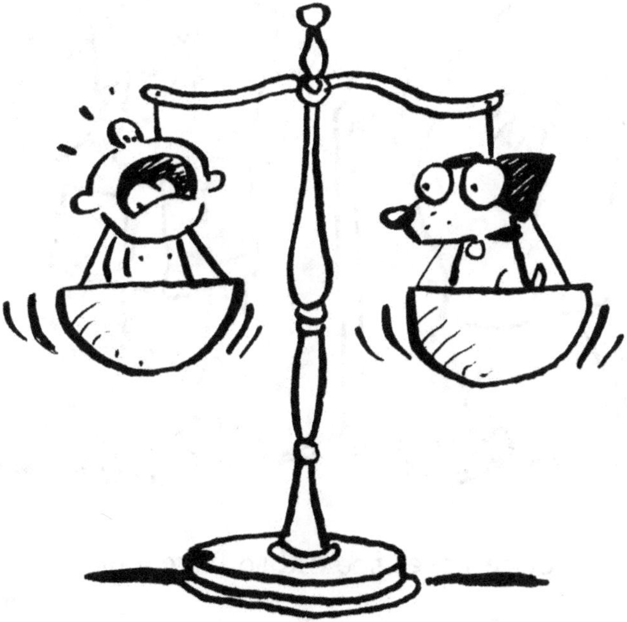

You're never too old to have a dog.

No one thinks you're unwise to get a dog on your own.

You don't have to give up drinking when you decide to get a dog.

You don't have to wear special clothing when you get a dog.

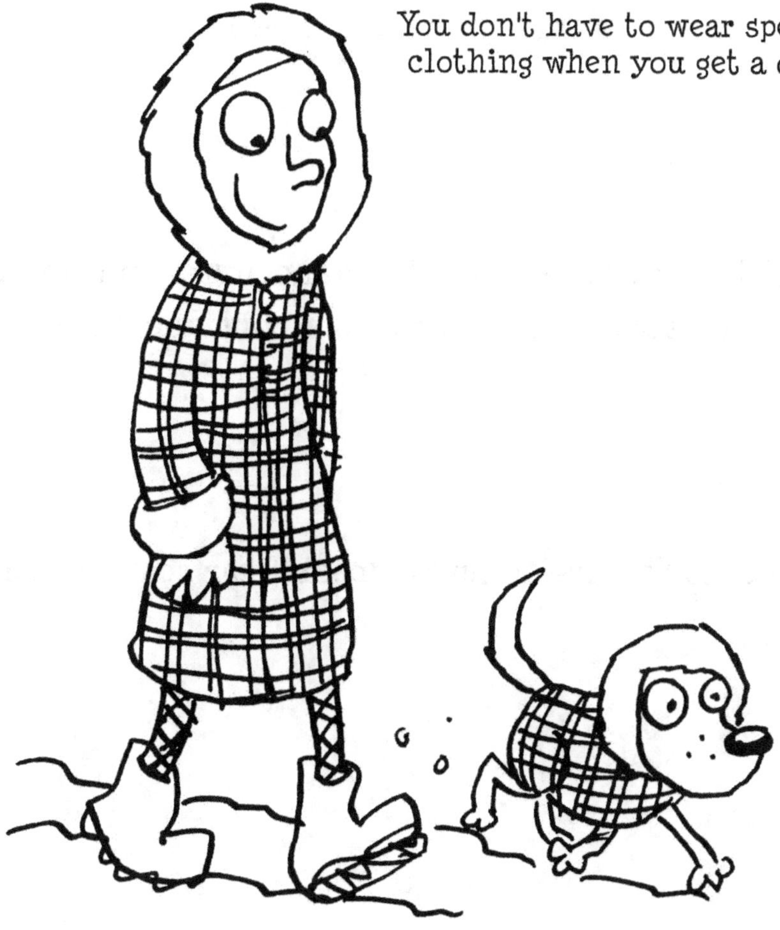

A dog won't give you morning sickness, swollen ankles or varicose veins.

You'll never have to try to manoeuvre your dog in an oversized pushchair into a boutique shop.

You don't have to buy a special car seat for a dog.

Getting a new dog rarely results in stitches.

The name you choose for your dog won't upset any relatives
(unless you call it something really rude).

You won't have trouble getting your figure back if you get a dog.

A dog won't wake you up in the middle of the night to be fed.

You won't feel guilty buying a dog food rather than breastfeeding it.

Dog-owners don't compare their dogs' developmental progress ad nauseum.

If you want to have a night out, you won't have to pay a fortune for a babysitter.

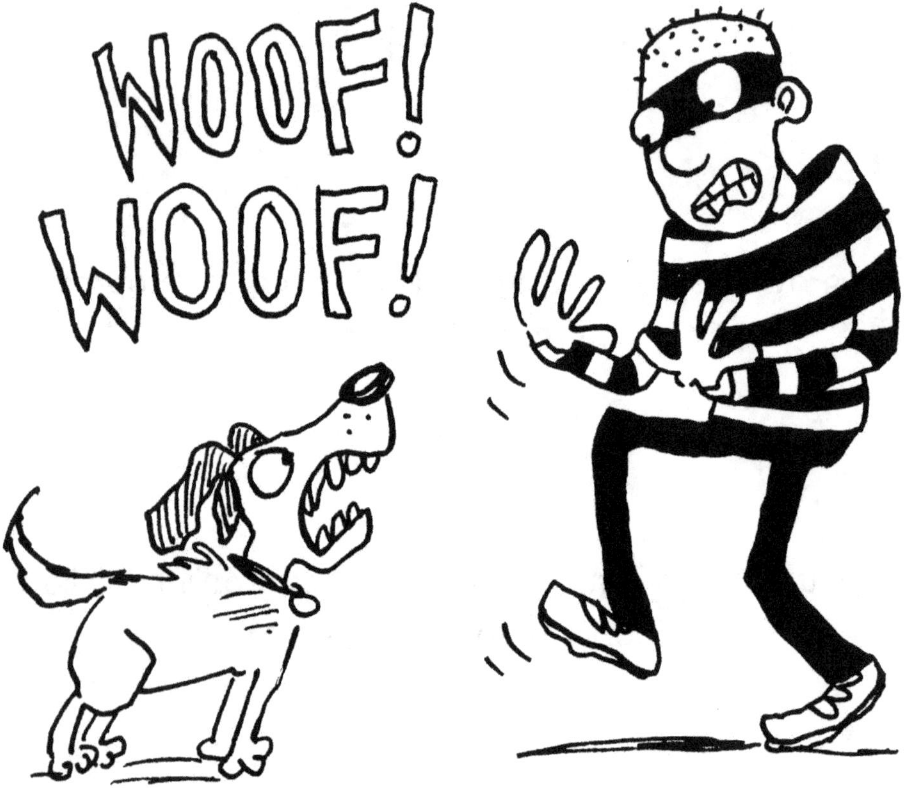
WOOF!
WOOF!

If a dog does wake you up in the middle of the night,
it will have a good reason.

Dog food doesn't have to be sterilised.

There's rarely any discussion about whether a dog looks more like you or your partner.

No matter how good your intentions, having a child really wrecks your eco-credentials.

There are more than ten times as many people as dogs in the world: dogs really are special.

Your dog won't outgrow its clothes/shoes every month or so.

A dog won't deprive you of sleep (yes, this has been written already, remember sleep deprivation is torture)

A dog won't develop a worrying rash every other day.

You never have to change a toxic nappy with a a dog (and it won't pee in your face).

A dog rarely needs a bath.

Your dog won't throw up down your favourite top.

You can be secure in the knowledge that your dog will never grow up to be a mass murderer...even if it would like to have a bloody good go at the squirrel population.

Toddler vs. Dog

You can leave your dog at home for 9 hours and no-one will call social services.

If you drop food on the floor, you're happy if your dog eats it.

A dog will rarely interrupt you when you are talking to a friend.

You don't have to worry about your dog drinking household bleach.

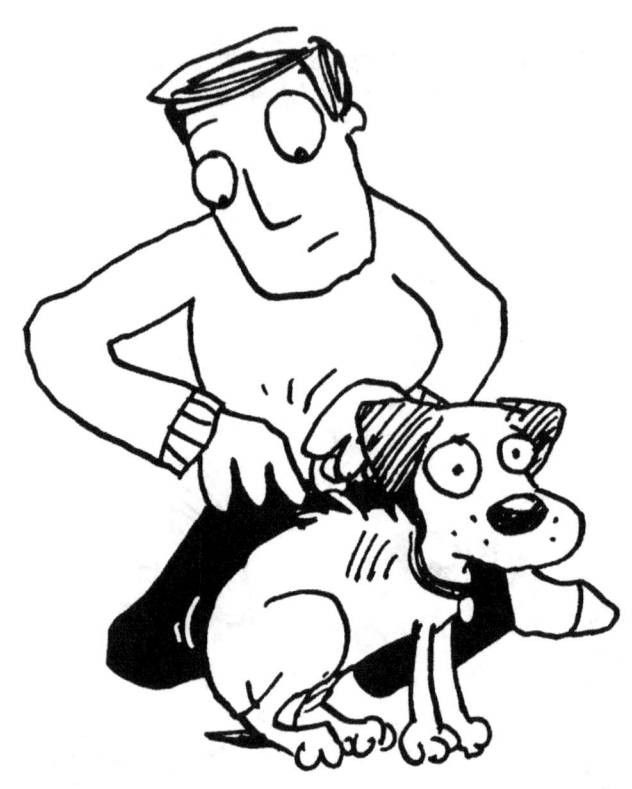

A dog won't get nits and you can give it medication for fleas, worms and ticks in advance.

If a dog doesn't finish his dinner, you know he's not well...

No-one moves house to get a dog into a good school.

Dogs don't have to have their noses wiped every other moment from colds they've caught from playschool.

If a dog bites someone, it can be put down.

A dog won't pester you to read it a story.

It never takes more than a year to housetrain a dog.

You can train a dog to obey your every command... for life.

You don't care if someone doesn't get the sex of your dog right.

Dogs don't generate mountains of laundry.

It's acceptable to give your dog only old tennis balls as its toys.

Dogs don't watch the same movie over and over and over again.

A dog won't hurl its dinner across the room.

Your dog will never poo in a public swimming pool.

A dog can't pick its nose (licking its bits is marginally more socially acceptable).

Dogs don't demand baby-cinos/fluffies or whatever the cafe wants to call them...

Your parents
won't buy your dog
unsuitable presents
every time they visit.

Dogs don't get sugar highs.

Dogs don't let on that you swear a lot in your house.

If you want to go to the movies, you won't need to pay through the nose for a babysitter on a Friday night.

It doesn't matter if your dog doesn't eat any vegetables.

Dogs can't scream.

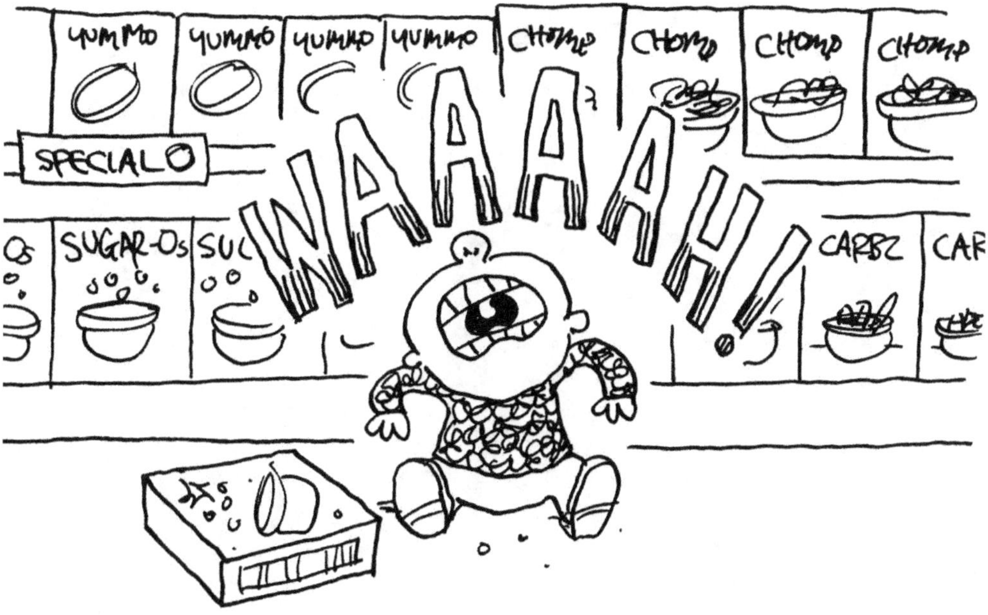
YUMMO
YUMMO
YUMMO
YUMMO
CHOMP
CHOMP
CHOMP
CHOMP
SPECIAL O
SUGAR-Os
WAAAAH!
CARBZ

Schoolkid vs. Dog

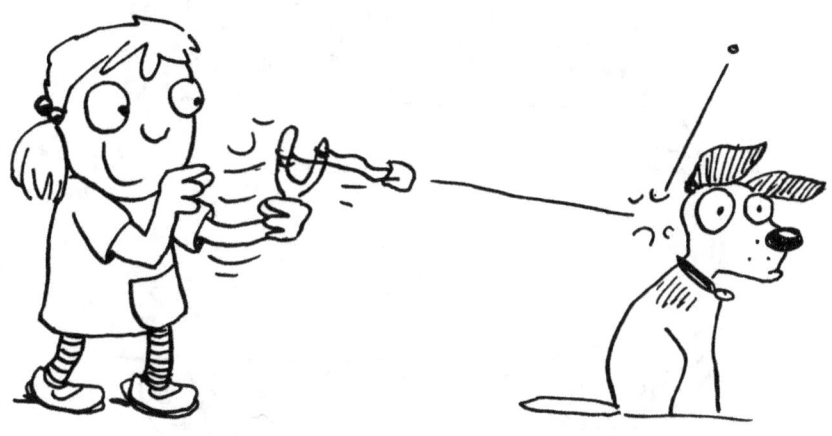

You can fit at least 6 dogs into the back of a compact car.

Dogs don't pick up every infection going to pass on to you.

You can't give a kid a bone from the butcher as its big treat.

You'll never need to teach your dog to ride a bicycle, but if you do, you could earn good money on YouTube.

Dogs won't pester you in the run up to their birthday/Christmas.

A dog finds it harder to open childproof medicine bottles than a child.

A dog cannot use
a water pistol.

You can't put a kid in kennels when you go on holiday.

A dog won't pester you for a smart phone.

You don't have to spend a lot of money on clothes for your dog.

Dogs don't get upset when they don't get picked for the soccer team.

It's okay for a dog to deliberately destroy its toys.

You know that paying for guitar lessons would be wasted on your dog.

A dog won't play graphically-disturbing computer games.

Kids never get excited about going on a long walk.

It's not cool to microchip a kid in case it gets lost, or stolen.

A dog won't accidentally reveal any family secrets to friends/teachers/complete strangers.

Your dog won't draw on another kid's face on a sleepover.

It's okay if dogs eat with their mouths open and they never talk with a mouthful of food.

Dogs never ask "Are we there yet?"

Dogs rarely steal anything other than food.

Dogs don't complain about their bedtime.

You don't have to worry that any fun your dog has outside is going to lead to 8 hours in hospital.

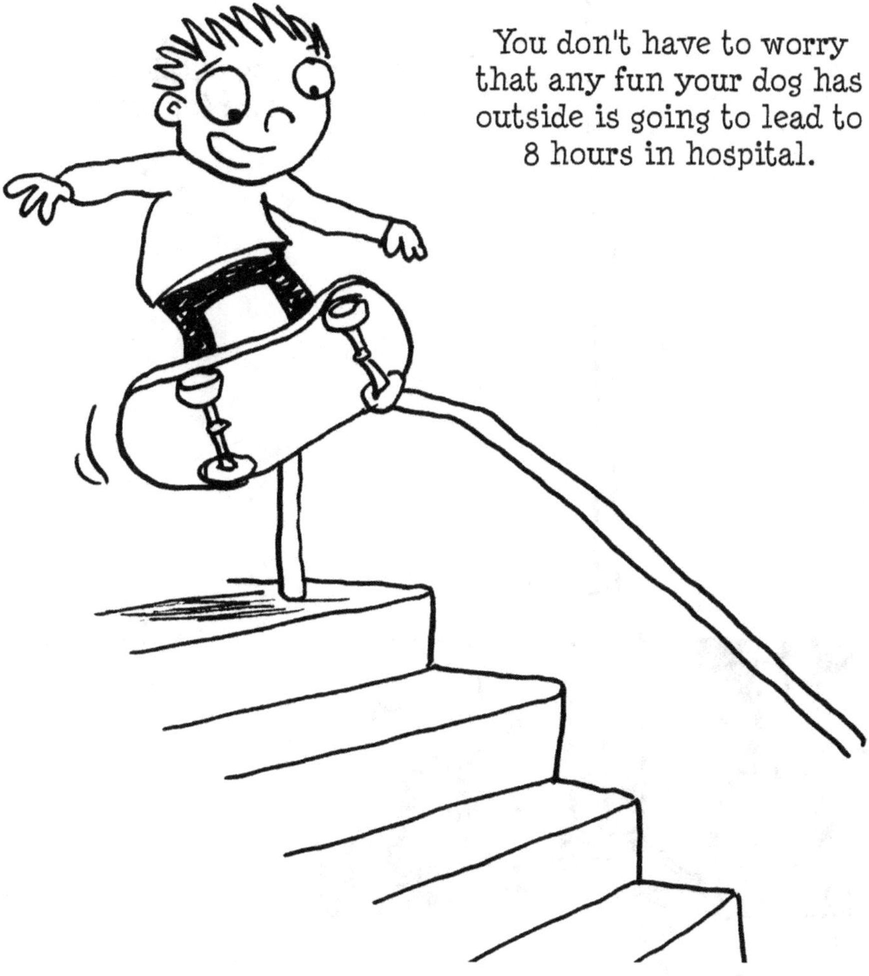

You can tie a dog outside when you go to a cafe for lunch.

You'll never have to help your dog with its homework.

Teenager vs. Dog

Dogs never argue with you.

At least not verbally.

Dogs love you unconditionally -
even if you don't buy them a iGadget.

Dogs cannot lie.

Your dog will never go out dressed inappropriately.

Your dog won't complain when you try to give it a hug.

A dog will never change the TV channel on you.

A dog won't empty the fridge on you.

A dog won't play its music so loud that you can't hear yourself speak.

You don't have to worry about your dog getting into drugs.

You'll never have to tell your dog it's spending too long in the bathroom.

Dogs don't run up huge phone bills.

Dogs don't send or receive dodgy phone messages.

Dogs rarely bring unsuitable girlfriends/boyfriends home.

You can always keep a dog on a lead.

A dog will give you a rapturous welcome every time you come home (even if you've only been out ten minutes).

Your dog will never buy itself a drum kit.

Dogs are happy with the same
  beds all their lives.

But it's not weird if a dog sleeps on your bed.

A dog doesn't complain that it's got nothing to wear.

If you get into difficulties, a dog is more likely to try and look after than you than a kid.

You don't have to worry about what a dog will see online.

You'll never have to give your dog driving lessons.

A dog never leaves dirty dishes in the sink.

A dog won't come home with its head shaved and tongue pierced.

You won't have to worry about your dog going to university or getting a job.

You don't have to re-mortgage your house to put a dog through college.

Epilogue

You know your dog won't be living with you when it's 30 years old.

THANK YOU FOR READING

I hope you enjoyed this book. As an independent author and illustrator it would really help me if you left a review for it on Amazon, or Goodreads. A single line is fine!

If you'd like to receive illustrated emails about other things I'm working on, please subscribe to my mailing list: http://eepurl.com/cCOOeD

ABOUT THE AUTHOR

Alex Hallatt was born and brought up in the West Country in England. She emigrated to New Zealand, where she met her partner, Duncan and his dog, Billie. They spent a few years living in Australia, England and Spain before moving back to New Zealand. Billie is buried under an apricot tree in their back garden.

You can see more of Alex's work at alexhallatt.com.

ALSO BY ALEX HALLATT

Arctic Circle Comics: An Introduction
Arctic Circle is about three penguins who have moved north. This cartoon collection introduces Oscar, Ed, Gordo and the other characters in this syndicated comic strip with an environmental theme.

The Book of Culls: The Best Human Cull Comics
A bumper collection of this tongue-in-cheek comic. Making the world a better place by removing all the really annoying people.

FAB (Friends Against Bullying) Club
For 8-12 year olds
If you were being bullied, what would you do? What if you could join a club that could make the bullying stop? This is the story of how the best ever club got started. Friends Against Bullying - Join the Club!

FAB Club 2
Friends Against Cyberbullying
For 8-12 year olds
When bullying happens everywhere and you can't escape, what can you do?
Will the FAB Club find a way to stand up to the cyberbullies?
Find out in FAB Club 2.

Hoover the Hungry Dog
For preschoolers
Hoover is always hungry and often eats things he shouldn't, with hilarious consequences.

www.ingramcontent.com/pod-product-compliance
Lightning Source LLC
Chambersburg PA
CBHW051150290426
44108CB00019B/2670